**Federal Aviation
Administration**

I0426377

DOT/FAA/AM-12/1
Office of Aerospace Medicine
Washington, DC 20591

Perceptions and Efficacy of Flight Operational Quality Assurance (FOQA) Programs Among Small-Scale Operators

Shelley E. Lowe
Elaine M. Pfleiderer
Thomas R. Chidester

Civil Aerospace Medical Institute
Federal Aviation Administration
Oklahoma City, OK 73125

January 2012

Final Report

OK-12-0025-JAH

NOTICE

This document is disseminated under the sponsorship
of the U.S. Department of Transportation in the interest
of information exchange. The United States Government
assumes no liability for the contents thereof.

_____

This publication and all Office of Aerospace Medicine technical reports are
available in full-text from the Civil Aerospace Medical Institute's publications
Web site:
www.faa.gov/library/reports/medical/oamtechreports/index.cfm

Technical Report Documentation Page

1. Report No. DOT/FAA/AM-12/1	2. Government Accession No.	3. Recipient's Catalog No.
4. Title and Subtitle Perceptions and Efficacy of Flight Operational Quality Assurance (FOQA) Programs Among Small-scale Operators		5. Report Date January 2012
		6. Performing Organization Code
7. Author(s) Lowe SE, Pfleiderer EM, Chidester TR		8. Performing Organization Report No.
9. Performing Organization Name and Address FAA Civil Aerospace Medical Institute P.O. Box 25082 Oklahoma City, OK 73125		10. Work Unit No. (TRAIS)
		11. Contract or Grant No.
12. Sponsoring Agency name and Address Office of Aerospace Medicine Federal Aviation Administration 800 Independence Ave., S.W. Washington, DC 20591		13. Type of Report and Period Covered
		14. Sponsoring Agency Code

15. Supplemental Notes

Work was accomplished under approved task HRR 521

16. Abstract

Despite safety and economic advantages, as well as endorsements by the International Civil Aviation Organization, the FAA, the National Transportation Safety Board, and Congress, voluntary Flight Operational Quality Assurance (FOQA) participation has not been fully implemented in the United States (GAO, 2010), particularly among small operators. Pilots' concern about data misuse continues to be one of the primary factors preventing participation in voluntary safety programs. Considered in conjunction with pilots' attitudes and pressure from pilot unions, airlines might find it difficult to justify the cost of implementing and maintaining a FOQA program if they are dubious about its benefits or concerned about its risks. Increased FOQA participation among small-scale air carriers may depend on demonstrating that significant safety benefits can be gained and positive perceptions of the program sustained, with minimal cost to the operator. The current study evaluates both attitudinal and operational aspects of a FOQA program maintained by a small-scale government aircraft operator. The Perceptions of Flight Operations Quality Assurance (PFOQA) questionnaire was used to systematically collect information about pilots' attitudes regarding FOQA. Questionnaire items were based on concerns and recommendations proposed by the Flight Safety Foundation FOQA task force created to identify issues that might hinder or prevent the implementation of FOQA. Survey participants were a sample of 83 government pilots drawn from a population of approximately 180 Office of Aviation System Standards (AJW) pilots. A time series analysis of FOQA event rates was used to determine whether quarterly reports providing feedback to pilots (a cost-effective intervention method) can produce significant safety benefits. FOQA exceedances used in the time series analyses were de-identified monthly summary data for the Learjet 60 fleet recorded between July 2006 and November 2010. The overlap between the distributions of the Positive and Negative Perceptions scales of the PFOQA suggests that the pilot group demonstrated a certain amount of ambivalence toward FOQA, recognizing both the value and risks of the program. The results of the time series analyses indicated that feedback provided to pilots in quarterly reports produced significant reductions in exceedance rates. A trend in the time series data was the pervasive reduction in these exceedances over the course of the program. This was encouraging for the AJW operation and should motivate other small operators to pursue FOQA.

17. Key Words Flight Operations Quality Assurance, FOQA, Voluntary Safety Programs, Time Series analysis	18. Distribution Statement Document is available to the public through the Defense Technical Information Center, Ft. Belvior, VA 22060; and the National Technical Information Service, Springfield, VA 22161		
19. Security Classif. (of this report) Unclassified	20. Security Classif. (of this page) Unclassified	21. No. of Pages 22	22. Price

Form DOT F 1700.7 (8-72) Reproduction of completed page authorized

ACKNOWLEDGMENTS

Research reported in this paper was conducted under the Flight Deck Program Directive/Level of Effort Agreement between the Human Factors Research and Engineering Group (AJP-61), FAA Headquarters, and the Aerospace Human Factors Research Division (AAM-500) of the Civil Aerospace Medical Institute. Special thanks are due to Ed Lucke (AJW-3) and Tom Pickle (AJW-38) for their support of this project, and to Tom Accardi (AJW-3, retired) for his many contributions to this research effort.

CONTENTS

Perceptions and Efficacy of Flight Operational Quality Assurance (FOQA) Programs Among Small-Scale Operators

The Flight Safety Foundation (FSF) defines Flight Operational Quality Assurance (FOQA) as a program "for obtaining and analyzing data recorded in flight to improve flight crew performance, air carrier training programs and operating procedures, airport maintenance and design, and aircraft operations and design" (Enders, 1993, p.1). For regulatory purposes, the Federal Aviation Administration (FAA) broadened the definition to include "routine collection and analysis of digital flight data gathered during aircraft operations" under Title 14 of the Code of Federal Regulations (CFR) Part 13.401.

FOQA programs evolved from accident investigation practices using Flight Data Recorders (FDRs), which were mandated in 1958 by the Civil Aeronautics Administration (the precursor to the FAA). Technological advances in data recording and improved data management capabilities enabled routine data analysis. FOQA programs use flight data from Quick Access Recorders (QARs) that can be easily downloaded from the aircraft and compiled for analysis. This allows operators to establish pre-determined unsafe parameters that will automatically flag events for review by supervisory and management personnel to improve pilot training, establish safer policies and standards, and lower operating costs.

FOQA data can also be used to "re-create" any flight for playback. Re-creation software provides three-dimensional views of aircraft movements, synchronized with recorded flight control and power lever readings. Cockpit instrument readings and switch positions are all displayed in chronologically-synchronized images from inside and outside the cockpit. When a potential safety threat is identified from a specific flight, regardless of whether or not it resulted in an incident, re-creations might help pilots better understand the lesson to be gained from FOQA data (Warwick, 2009).

As indicated by a report published by the U.S. Government Accountability Office (GAO) in 1997, FOQA programs not only enhance safety but also provide economic benefits because airlines actively participating in FOQA are "better able to achieve optimum fuel consumption and avoid unneeded engine maintenance. Although more difficult to quantify, enhanced safety should result in lower costs over time as a result of accidents avoided and lower insurance premiums" (GAO, 1997, p.2). Despite safety and economic advantages, as well as endorsements by the International Civil Aviation Organization (ICAO), the FAA, the National Transportation Safety Board (NTSB), and Congress, not all U.S. operators have chosen to participate in FOQA programs (GAO, 2010). Participation in FOQA is particularly low among small operators.[1]

Prior to FOQA adoption in the United States, the FSF formed a FOQA task force to identify issues that might hinder or prevent its implementation. Recognizing that data security was critical, a special working group was created from within the FOQA task force to concentrate on these issues. The working group identified two main areas of concern: that data in the possession of the federal government could be released in response to Freedom of Information Act (FOIA) requests or through civil litigation, and that information from FOQA data could be used in enforcement or disciplinary actions against pilots.

Pilots' concerns about enforcement or disciplinary actions were not unfounded. En route air traffic controllers have been electronically monitored since the Operational Error Detection Patch (OEDP) was deployed more than 20 years ago. The OEDP alerts area managers when a loss of separation standards has occurred (whereas previous versions of the software only alerted the controller that loss of separation may be imminent). Management then determines who was responsible for the loss of separation (Schroeder, Bailey, Pounds, & Manning, 2006). If responsibility for loss of separation is assigned to air traffic control, it is classified as an operational error. If the pilot is found to be responsible, it is classified as a pilot deviation. Although the OEDP was ostensibly created as a means of minimizing operational errors, it has routinely been used for disciplinary purposes (Miller, 1986). A pilot deviation can result in an enforcement action against the pilot and possible license suspension. That controllers and pilots refer to the OEDP as the "snitch patch" is an indication of their attitude toward the program.

Two federal regulations were adopted to address these issues. The first prohibits the FAA from using data obtained from an approved FOQA program for the purpose of enforcement action against an operator or its employees, except in the case of criminal or deliberate acts (14 CFR §13.401). The second provides that voluntarily-submitted information will not be disclosed by the FAA in response to a FOIA request (14 CFR §193). Disciplinary action within an airline is not addressed

---

[1]The GAO (2010) defines "small carriers" as those with less than 5,000,000 enplaned passengers annually, whereas "large carriers" are defined as the top 25 U.S. carriers with 5,000,000 or more passengers annually.

by the regulation and must be addressed by company/union agreement permitting FOQA data collection. The disclosure of FOQA data through civil litigation remains a risk because the FAA cannot restrict the authority of courts through regulation, and legal precedents have been mixed (GAO, 1997). Airlines and pilot groups that have supported FOQA have made a risk-based judgment that learning about and addressing risks mitigates and outweighs legal risks of collecting the information. They view it as clearly better and more defensible to know and act than to avoid risk of knowledge.

Research results of electronic monitoring in other fields suggest that perceptions of intended data use greatly influence employees' attitudes about data collection. Procedural justice is important for the acceptance of any new procedure and often determines its success (e.g., Konovsky & Cropanzo, 1991; Ambrose & Alder, 2000; Douthitt & Aiello, 2002). Westin (1992) concluded that employees' perceptions of the fairness of performance standards and measurement processes and a prevailing climate of organizational trust were important factors. Unfortunately, uneven protections under the federal regulations and prevailing attitudes about the OEDP (a/k/a "snitch patch") render establishing a sense of procedural justice and organizational trust problematic.

Fortunately, the combined efforts of the FAA and the airline industry have produced procedural guidelines for protecting FOQA data and engendering trust in the program. An Advisory Circular (AC No. 120-82) published by the FAA in 2004 provides a best practices model for developing, implementing, and operating FOQA programs that will qualify for FAA approval. This document emphasizes the importance of focusing on identifying trends from aggregated data (as opposed to using data gathered during a single flight) and cautions that information identifying flight crew members should be removed as part of the initial processing of the airborne data. It also provides guidance for establishing a gatekeeper who may be provided with identifying information for a limited period of time, should crew contact be necessary for the purpose of collecting contextual information or describing special circumstances associated with a particular event.

A recent report by the GAO (2010) stated that the majority of Part 121[2] flights are currently operated by airlines with FAA-approved FOQA programs, but only 17% of the smaller carriers have them. According to this report, pilots' concerns about data misuse continues to be one of the primary factors that prevent their participation in voluntary safety programs. This mainly applies to voluntary reporting programs, such as the Aviation

Safety Action Program (ASAP), but may impact FOQA as well. Considered in conjunction with pilots' attitudes and pressure from pilot unions, airlines might find it difficult to justify the cost of implementing and maintaining a FOQA program if they are dubious about its benefits or concerned about its risks. Increased FOQA participation among small-scale air carriers might depend on demonstrating that significant safety benefits can be gained, and positive perceptions of the program sustained, with minimal cost to the operator.

As mentioned previously, both pilots' attitudes and financial considerations have been cited as potential factors preventing the implementation of FOQA programs among small-scale operators. Therefore, the current study addresses both attitudinal and operational aspects of FOQA programs.

Experiment 1 evaluates pilots' perceptions of a FOQA program maintained by a small-scale government operator. The Office of Aviation System Standards (AJW) employs approximately 180 pilots and operates within strict budgetary constraints. As such, this organization faces many of the same challenges as comparable small-scale commercial operators. The FOQA program at AJW has been fully operational since 2006, and so pilots' experience and attitudes about FOQA should be well developed in this group. To date, reports of pilots' perceptions of FOQA programs have been largely based on anecdotal evidence. In the present study, we used a previously-validated survey instrument (Pfleiderer & Chidester, 2011) to systematically collect information about pilots' attitudes regarding FOQA.

Experiment 2 examines operational efficacy using time series analysis. Trends suggesting improved pilot performance may simply be a function of monitoring alone, or might represent a natural progression over the course of time. Time series analysis removes systematic trends so the actual effects of interventions may be evaluated. Time series analysis of FOQA event rates should determine whether quarterly reports providing feedback to pilots (a cost-effective intervention method) can produce significant safety benefits.

EXPERIMENT 1

Method

Participants. Survey participants were a sample of 83 government pilots drawn from a population of approximately 180 AJW pilots working at one of six base office locations (see Table 1). In response to categorical items concerning their experience with FOQA, 7 of the pilots indicated that they had participated on an event review committee or as FOQA program administrators, 31 had

---

[2]Title 14 Part 121 of the Code of Federal Regulations governs scheduled air carriers.

Table 1. PFOQA Survey Participants: Base of Operations

Base Location	Number of Pilot Participants
Atlantic City, NJ	8
Anchorage, AK	2
Atlanta, GA	8
Battle Creek, MI	13
Oklahoma City, OK	32
Sacramento, CA	14
Unknown	6
Total	**83**

read industry articles about FOQA, 54 had attended briefings or formal training regarding FOQA programs, and 54 had served as flight crew members on an aircraft actively participating in a FOQA program. Of the 54 pilots who served as FOQA flight crew members, 10 had served less than three years, 28 had served between three and five years, and 9 had served more than five years. (The remaining 7 failed to provide information about the amount of time they had served on aircraft actively participating in FOQA programs.) Though many participants failed to respond to categorical items about their experience with FOQA, all were currently serving as flight crew members for AJW. Therefore, all had experience serving as flight crew members on aircraft actively participating in a FOQA program at the time the survey was conducted.

Measures. The Perceptions of Flight Operations Quality Assurance (PFOQA) questionnaire was developed by co-authors Thomas R. Chidester (Manager of the FAA Aerospace Human Factors Research Division) and Thomas C. Accardi (former Director of FAA Aviation System Standards) to elicit pilots' level of agreement with a series of statements about FOQA programs, using a format widely recognized as one of the best for collecting information about attitudes (Nunnally, 1978). Questionnaire items were based on the concerns and recommendations proposed by the FSF FOQA task force created to identify issues that might hinder or prevent the implementation of FOQA programs in this country (GAO, 1997). The PFOQA online questionnaire completed by the pilots consisted of 16 Likert-type items, a few demographic items, and one open-ended question (*Please tell us anything else you think we should know about your expectations or concerns about FOQA*) located at the end of the survey to allow identification of issues not included among the existing items (see Appendix A).

The 16 items of the PFOQA questionnaire were intended to represent two scale dimensions: Positive Perceptions and Negative Perceptions. The Positive Perceptions Scale comprised expectations and beliefs about positive safety enhancements of FOQA programs. Items in the Negative Perceptions Scale addressed data misuse and organizational trust issues. Cronbach's alpha is a measure of internal consistency reliability. By convention, a minimum Cronbach's alpha of .80 is required for a "good" scale (Nunnally, 1978). The 9-item Positive Perceptions Scale (α=.86) and the 7-item Negative Perceptions Scale (α=.88) both demonstrated good internal consistency in a sample of 199 commercial pilots (Pfleiderer & Chidester, 2011). Nevertheless, individual item test results (e.g., squared multiple correlations from regression equations using each item as the dependent variable, with all other items as predictors) were lower than preferred for some of the PFOQA questions. These items also failed to load consistently with their hypothesized dimensions in Principal Components Analysis (for a detailed description, see Pfleiderer & Chidester, 2011).

Though Cronbach's alpha is extremely sensitive to the number of items in a scale (i.e., fewer items generally reduce alpha), elimination of the problematic items actually increased alpha. The 6-item Positive Perceptions Scale and 6-item Negative Perceptions Scale (Table 2) produced alphas of .88 and .91, respectively. In addition, Principal Components Analysis (Appendix B) verified that the remaining 12 items produced a two-component solution that accounted for more variance than a model constructed from the original 16 items. Therefore, scale scores were computed from a reduced set of 12 items, rather than the full set of 16 items.

Procedure. Online PFOQA survey data collection was conducted from 2/24/2010 to 4/28/2010. The invitation to participate and a URL for the online survey were provided in a memorandum (see Appendix C) that was only disseminated to flight operations personnel. Unfortunately, participant confidentiality precluded taking measures to prevent pilots from responding more than once.

Table 2. *Perceptions of Flight Operations Quality Assurance (PFOQA) Questionnaire Scale Items*

Positive Perceptions Scale (6 Items, α = .88)
01 FOQA is a program designed to enhance safety by identifying potential hazards before they result in an accident.
04 Flying skills have improved or will improve with a FOQA program in place.
06 I expect FOQA data to be used to take action to correct safety problems.
07 I expect FOQA data to be used to improve pilot training.
11 I expect FOQA data to provide our pilot group with useful feedback on our performance.
13 I expect the FOQA program to positively impact the safety of our operations.
Negative Perceptions Scale (6 Items, α = .91)
03 (Reflected) I trust management will not misuse FOQA data against individual pilots.
05 I worry that FOQA data will be a source of information for enforcement action against pilots.
09 I worry that FOQA data will be used for disciplinary actions.
14 A FOQA program has negatively impacted, or will negatively impact, the morale of our pilots.
15 I worry that FOQA data could be released under the Freedom of Information Act.
16 I worry that FOQA data could be released through civil litigation.

NOTE: In the computation of the Negative Perceptions Scale, Item 03 is scored as if it were written in reverse (i.e., "I don't trust management...").

Results and Discussion

Summary descriptive statistics for the PFOQA survey items are shown in Table 3. Frequencies and proportions for individual PFOQA items are provided in Appendix D. Likert-type scales perform reasonably well in parametric analyses when there are five or more categories (Johnson & Creech, 1983; Zumbo & Zimmerman, 1993), but a standard normal distribution in the population cannot be assumed with a 4-point scale (e.g., Berry, 1993). Even so, none of the distributions was in excess of three standard deviations from normality in either skewness or kurtosis. It could be argued that the PFOQA items might constitute a 5-point scale if "No Opinion" responses were coded as if they represented moderate agreement. However, having no opinion is not the same as having a moderate one. "No Opinion" responses were coded as missing for the analysis of individual items, and item means were substituted for "No Opinion" values in the computation of scale scores.

Positive Perceptions and Negative Perceptions scales represent the sum of response items associated with each of the two dimensions (see Table 2). Distributions of composite Positive and Negative Perceptions Scale scores computed from the PFOQA items are shown in Figure 1. Higher values on the computed Positive and Negative Perceptions scales reflect higher overall levels of agreement with the underlying dimensions (i.e., higher levels of agreement with negative items results in a higher Negative Perceptions Scale score, higher levels of agreement with positive items results in a higher Positive Perceptions Scale score.) Not surprisingly, there was a statistically significant inverse relationship between participants' Positive and Negative Perceptions scale scores ($r = -.56$, $p<.01$). That is to say, individuals with higher Positive Perceptions Scale scores tended to have lower Negative Perceptions Scale scores and vice versa, though there was considerable overlap between the distributions. There was also greater variance of opinion within the Negative Perceptions Scale, which had a bimodal distribution with visible peaks on either side of the median scale score of 15.00.

The overlap between the distributions of the Positive and Negative Perceptions scales suggests a coexistence of positive and negative feelings about FOQA (i.e., pilots believed in the FOQA program overall but remained concerned about various issues). From this perspective, the group did not appear to be neutral about FOQA. Rather, they demonstrated a certain amount of ambivalence, recognizing both the value and risks of the program. This is reflected in relatively high mean scores for both the Positive and Negative Perception scales (18.72 versus 15.72), though pilots endorsed the positive items more

Table 3. *Perceptions of Flight Operations Quality Assurance (PFOQA) Questionnaire Items: Descriptive Statistics*

PFOQA Item	n	No Opinion	System Missing	Mean	SD	Skewness	Kurtosis
01 FOQA is a program designed to enhance safety by identifying potential hazards....	82	1	0	3.44	.59	-.50	-.64
02 Gatekeepers are the only persons able to access identifying information that....	78	5	0	2.90	.92	-.61	-.32
03 I trust management will not misuse FOQA data against individual pilots.	79	4	0	2.71	1.00	-.32	-.92
04 Flying skills have improved or will improve with a FOQA program in place.	79	4	0	2.73	.87	-.40	-.40
05 I worry that FOQA data will be a source of information for enforcement action....	80	3	0	2.45	.88	.10	-.66
06 I expect FOQA data to be used to take action to correct safety problems.	81	2	0	3.28	.62	-.59	1.16
07 I expect FOQA data to be used to improve pilot training.	82	1	0	3.11	.67	-.38	.27
08 I expect FOQA data to be used to optimize maintenance.	69	13	1	2.81	.88	-.42	-.41
09 I worry that FOQA data will be used for disciplinary actions.	78	3	2	2.44	.88	-.04	-.67
10 I expect FOQA data to be used to change cockpit procedures.	79	4	0	3.15	.51	.25	.53
11 I expect FOQA data to provide our pilot group with useful feedback on our....	82	0	1	3.04	.78	-.71	.55
12 I expect FOQA data to be used to change procedures outside our organization....	67	15	1	2.04	.77	.55	.29
13 I expect the FOQA program to positively impact the safety of our operations.	79	4	0	3.11	.66	-.67	1.48
14 A FOQA program has negatively impacted, or will negatively impact, the morale....	77	6	0	2.25	.81	.57	.06
15 I worry that FOQA data could be released under the Freedom of Information Act.	72	11	0	2.69	.80	-.24	-.28
16 I worry that FOQA data could be released through civil litigation.	72	10	1	2.90	.77	-.40	-.04

Note: Individual items were coded 1 = Strongly Disagree, 2 = Disagree, 3 = Agree, 4 = Strongly Agree

than the negative items. Positive Perception Scale scores were more normally distributed than those of the Negative Perceptions Scale. In fact, the Negative Perception Scale scores had a bimodal distribution. In other words, approximately half of the sample (51%) appeared to disagree with most of the items in the Negative Perceptions Scale, and the other half (49%) agreed with most of them.

A closer examination of the individual questionnaire items among pilots with high Negative Perceptions Scale scores (i.e., the 49% with scores above the median) permitted identification of particular issues concerning a significant portion of the pilot group. Four of the items suggest issues that could be addressed in the sampled pilot group and which may generalize to other small operators. Most of

this sub-group (95%) expressed concern about FOQA data being released through civil litigation. This perception of vulnerability to civil litigation is not without justification. As noted earlier, court rulings thus far have varied regarding FOQA data. For example, in a 1995 case involving a major U.S. air carrier, the federal district court for the District of South Carolina[3] ruled that voluntarily collected safety data were not protected under the self-critical evaluation privilege. Just a few years later, the federal district court for the Southern District of Florida[4] also rejected the claim of

[3] In re: Air Crash at Charlotte, North Carolina on July 2, 1994, 982 F. Supp. 1052 (D.S.C. 1997).
[4] In re: Air Crash Near Cali, Columbia on December 20, 1995, 959 F. Supp. 1529 (S.D. Fla 1997).

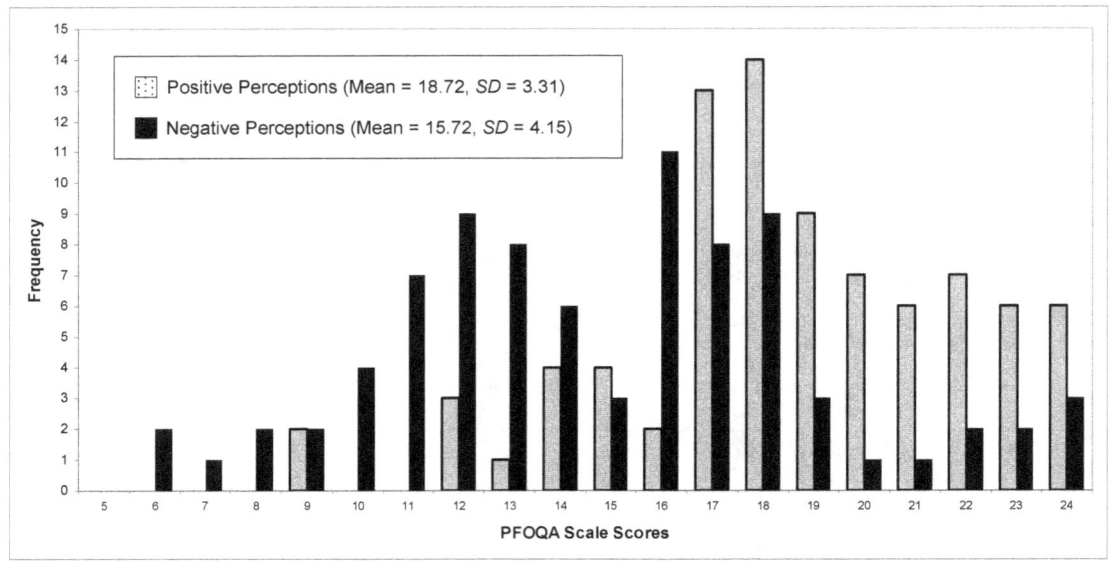

Figure 1. Frequency Distributions of Perceptions of Flight Operations Quality Assurance (PFOQA) Scale Scores

self-critical evaluation, but recognized a new qualified privilege and did not compel the air carrier to disclose the data.

A similar trend regarding FOIA release is somewhat less rational. Approximately 85% of pilots with high Negative Perceptions Scale scores (54% of the total sample) indicated they were concerned about FOQA data being released under the Freedom of Information Act, despite the fact that regulatory action (14 CFR §193) has addressed this concern well. This might indicate a general lack of knowledge about FOIA or that the success of government actions had not been effectively communicated to the pilot group, thus representing an opportunity for improvement in communication that may generalize to other operators.

Likewise, 85% of the pilots with high Negative Perceptions Scale scores (46% of the total sample) indicated that they were concerned about FOQA data being used for disciplinary actions. The validity of this perception depends upon specific agreements negotiated between the operator and the pilot group. In the case of AJW, protections against disciplinary action using FOQA data are extremely strong. Therefore, pilots' apprehensions may reflect concerns about people rather than processes. Although the pilots may trust the current gatekeeper, they may harbor misgivings about any future, and therefore unknown, gatekeepers. For any given operator, this finding implies that communication about flight crew protections against disciplinary actions using FOQA data is a key issue.

Disappointingly, approximately 83% of the pilots with high Negative Perceptions Scale scores (45% of the total sample) worried that FOQA data will be used for enforcement actions. This is an area where the FAA has

perhaps taken its strongest stand (14 CFR §13.401) and for which an industry history of honoring those protections has been clearly demonstrated. This signals that the issue is so important that organizations should strive to consistently remind pilots of regulatory protections and make sure that every demonstration of compliance is communicated to them.

The Negative Perception items regarding trust in management (68%) and a potential negative impact on morale (58%) appear to be of slightly less importance to the sub-group of pilots with high Negative Perceptions Scale scores. This lack of concern is even more pronounced in the full sample. Only 36% indicated mistrust that management might use FOQA data against individual pilots, and only 28% thought FOQA might have had a negative impact on morale. As has been reported elsewhere in the management research literature, this group trusts the management personnel closest to them (i.e., their immediate supervisors in AJW) more than they trust the distant personnel responsible for enforcement (i.e., FAA Office of Flight Standards) or the courts.

EXPERIMENT 2

Method

Flight Operational Quality Assurance (FOQA) event exceedance rates. FOQA events are predetermined conditions that can be monitored during various phases of flight. Event sets are customized for a particular organization (e.g., fleet aircraft type limitations, company operational procedures) and are limited by the availability of measured parameters on the aircraft. An exceedance occurs when analysis verifies that an aircraft was operated outside established event

Table 4. *Autocorrelation Functions (ACF) and Box-Ljung Statistics by FOQA Event*

Rate of Descent High (400-1200 ft. AGL)						Speed High Below 10,000 ft.					
Lag	ACF	S.E.	Box-Ljung			Lag	ACF	S.E.	Box-Ljung		
			Value	df	Sig.*				Value	df	Sig.*
1	-.05	.14	.13	1	.72	1	-.07	.13	.23	1	.63
2	-.06	.13	.35	2	.84	2	-.13	.13	1.19	2	.55
3	.12	.13	1.11	3	.77	3	-.02	.13	1.21	3	.75
4	-.22	.13	4.01	4	.41	4	.01	.13	1.22	4	.88
5	.02	.13	4.04	5	.54	5	-.17	.13	2.88	5	.72
6	.17	.13	5.71	6	.46	6	-.03	.13	2.93	6	.82
7	.00	.13	5.71	7	.57	7	.09	.13	3.46	7	.84
8	-.15	.13	7.07	8	.53	8	.02	.13	3.49	8	.90
9	.08	.12	7.50	9	.58	9	-.11	.12	4.26	9	.89
10	-.09	.12	7.98	10	.63	10	-.01	.12	4.27	10	.93
11	.07	.12	8.35	11	.68	11	-.04	.12	4.36	11	.96
12	.10	.12	9.03	12	.70	12	.05	.12	4.52	12	.97
13	-.20	.12	11.77	13	.55	13	-.02	.12	4.55	13	.98
14	.09	.12	12.33	14	.58	14	-.04	.12	4.65	14	.99
15	-.12	.12	13.41	15	.57	15	.15	.11	6.43	15	.97
16	-.06	.11	13.67	16	.62	16	.14	.11	8.06	16	.95

* Based on the asymptotic chi-square approximation.

parameters. FOQA exceedances used in the time series analyses were de-identified monthly summary data for the Learjet 60 fleet recorded between July 2006 and November 2010. Exceedances were adjusted for the number of flights within the series (i.e., rates rather than frequencies) to ensure that all were in the same metric. Though AJW monitors approximately 53 unique FOQA events, analysis was limited to two of the most prevalent exceedances with stable parameters (i.e., the event criteria weren't revised during the data collection period): *Rate of Descent High (400-1200 feet AGL)* and *Speed High Below 10,000 feet.*

Results and Discussion

In time series analysis, data are statistically modeled to remove the lingering effects of previous scores, general trends, and the effects of preceding random errors. Once outside sources of systematic variation have been removed, interventions may be tested to determine whether they have an effect (i.e., interrupted time-series analysis). Data for the interrupted time series analysis consisted of 53 monthly summary FOQA exceedance rates.[5] These were based on a total of 5,194 flights (Mean = 98; SD = 22.30) occurring between July 2006 and November 2010. Interventions were Aviation System Standards FOQA/ASAP Quarterly Releases that were disseminated to pilots throughout the data collection period. Only releases that specifically referenced the event sets being analyzed (i.e., *Rate of Descent High 400-1200 feet* and *Speed High Below 10,000 feet*) were coded as interventions.

The first step in interrupted time-series analysis is to identify and remove pre-existing, systematic patterns that cannot logically be attributed to the effect of an intervention, leaving only "white noise" after all systematic variance has been removed. Therefore, successful modeling is reflected by a lack of significant autocorrelations among the residuals. Model identification was expedited by the IBM SPSS 19.0 Time Series Modeler. The "Expert Modeler" automatically identifies and estimates the best-fitting Auto-regressive Integrated Moving Average (ARIMA) model for the data, eliminating the need to identify an appropriate model through trial and error alone. In some cases, the procedure suggested a model that failed to adequately fit the data. In these instances, parameter adjustments were made, following recommendations by Tabachnick and Fidell (2006), until a satisfactory model was identified. Each model is customized to the particular distribution to ensure that no systematic variance remains. Model evaluation was accomplished by examination of autocorrelation and partial autocorrelation functions. Significance values of the Box-Ljung statistic at each lag indicate the probability that the observed autocorrelation is random. As shown in Table 4, no significant autocorrelations remained, indicating that sequential contingencies had been removed by the selected model parameters.

---

[5]One of the cornerstones of a successful FOQA program is data confidentiality. Therefore, summary data for monthly FOQA exceedance rates are not reported.

Table 5. *ARIMA Parameter Estimates for Monthly Exceedance Rates (N = 53)*

Rate of Descent High (400-1200 ft. AGL)					
ARIMA (1,2,0)		Estimates	S.E.	*t*	Approx. Sig.
Non-Seasonal Lags	Auto-Regression	-.875	.077	-11.07	.00
Regression Coefficients	Release 09/01/2006	-.116	.040	-2.86	**.01**
	Release 12/15/2006	.013	.031	.42	.68
	Release 05/01/2007	-.087	.031	-2.82	**.01**
	Release 08/01/2007	.010	.031	.34	.74
	Release 11/01/2007	-.017	.031	-.56	.58
	Release 02/01/2008	-.061	.031	-1.99	**.05**
	Release 05/01/2008	-.074	.031	-2.39	**.02**
	Release 08/01/2008	-.071	.031	-2.31	**.03**
	Release 11/01/2008	.010	.031	.34	.74
	Release 02/01/2009	.010	.031	.31	.76
	Release 05/01/2009	-.007	.031	-.23	.82
Speed High Below 10,000 ft.					
ARIMA (1,1,0)		Estimates	S.E.	*t*	Approx. Sig.
Non-Seasonal Lags	Auto-Regression	-.497	.138	-3.61	.00
Regression Coefficients	Release 09/01/2006	-.068	.025	-2.67	**.01**
	Release 12/15/2006	-.002	.025	-.08	.93
	Release 05/01/2007	-.026	.025	-1.04	.31
	Release 08/01/2008	.031	.025	1.20	.24
	Release 02/01/2009	-.056	.025	-2.20	**.03**
	Release 08/01/2009	-.018	.025	-.71	.48
	Release 11/01/2009	-.006	.025	-.22	.83
	Release 05/01/2010	-.037	.025	-1.46	.15
	Release 08/01/2010	-.030	.025	-1.18	.24

Melard's algorithm was used for estimation.

In general, ARIMA models address three potential sources of systematic variation in a series. As shown in Table 5, auto-regressive parameters (i.e., lingering effects of previous scores) differed significantly from zero ($p < .01$) for both models. This is not surprising as interventions were part of a feedback loop. Quarterly releases reported increases in exceedance rates occurring within the previous quarter, so it makes sense that there would be lingering effects from previous rates. Both series also required differencing to compensate for steady downward linear trends in exceedance rates (i.e., integrated elements) since FOQA implementation. Neither series demonstrated the effects of preceding random errors (i.e., moving averages).

Once satisfactory models of pre-intervention data were identified, it was possible to test the effects of interventions on the subsequent data series. Table 5 contains parameter estimates, standard errors, *t*-tests, and approximate significance values for both models. Positive beta parameter estimates indicate increased exceedance rates. Increases were relatively rare in both series, and none was statistically significant. Negative beta parameter estimates indicate that exceedance rates were reduced following pilot feedback. Most of the parameter estimates showed decreases, and several were statistically significant. Interventions were evaluated as step (as opposed to pulse) functions. Coding interventions as step functions requires that changes must be persistent (as opposed to transitory) to achieve statistical significance.

SUMMARY AND CONCLUDING DISCUSSION

Though research results on the relationship between employee perceptions and job performance have been equivocal (e.g., Panina, 2002), AJW pilots' faith that feedback was working is supported by the time series analyses. Overall, the results indicate that feedback provided to pilots in Quarterly Releases produced significant, persistent reductions in exceedance rates. It is important to note that the two event sets submitted to analysis represent a small sample of all possible FOQA event sets. Other types of events may not respond as well to simple feedback reports (i.e., some might require flight simulation or intense classroom training). Further research is required to determine whether or not these results generalize to other event sets.

Still, the overwhelming reduction trend in exceedance rates of these events over the course of the time series was impressive. Simply by measuring selected flight parameters, informing pilots what had been observed, explaining why exceedances represented an unacceptable risk, and recommending strategies for avoiding these circumstances, AJW pilots were able to profoundly and quickly reduce the frequency of these events. This is remarkable because it only required measurement and feedback (i.e., issues endorsed by pilots in the Positive

Perceptions scale). It did *not* require identification of individual pilots, disciplinary action, or public disclosure of findings (i.e., concerns reported by pilots on the Negative Perceptions scale) to bring about this change. This accomplishment should motivate other small operators to consider FOQA programs.

REFERENCES

Ambrose, M.L., & Alder, G.S. (2000). Designing, implementing, and utilizing computerized performance monitoring: enhancing organizational justice. *Research in Personnel and Human Recourse Management, 18*, 187-219.

Berry, W.D. (1993). *Understanding regression assumptions.* Quantitative Applications in the Social Sciences, No. 92. Thousand Oaks, CA: Sage.

Code of Federal Regulations, Title 14, Part 13. Washington, DC: U.S. Government Printing Office, 2010.

Douthitt, E.A., & Aiello, J.R. (2001). The role of participation and control in the effects of computer monitoring on fairness perceptions, task satisfaction, and performance. *Journal of Applied Psychology, 86*, 867-874.

Enders, J.H. (April 1993). Study urges application of flight operational quality assurance methods in U.S. air carrier operations. *Flight Safety Digest*, 1-13.

Flight Safety Foundation (2004, June-July). Wealth of guidance and experience encourage wider adoption of FOQA. *Flight Safety Digest,* 1-22.

Government Accountability Office (1997). *Aviation safety: Efforts to implement flight operational quality assurance programs.* (Report No. GAO/RCED-98-10). Washington, DC: Author.

Government Accountability Office (2010). *Aviation safety: Improved data quality and analysis capabilities are needed as FAA plans a risk-based approach to safety oversight.* (Report No. GAO/RCED-10-414). Washington, DC: Author.

Johnson, D.R., & Creech, J.C. (1983). Ordinal measures in multiple indicator models: A simulation study of categorization error. *American Sociological Review, 48*, 398-407.

Konovsky, M., & Cropanzano, R. (1991). Perceived fairness of employee drug testing as a predictor of employee attitudes and job performance. *Journal of Applied Psychology, 76*, 698-707.

McNall, L.A., & Roch, S.G. (2009) A social exchange model of employee relations to electronic monitoring. *Human Performance, 22*, 209-224.

Miller, J.J. (1986, December) Separation strategies—computer cop. *AOPA Pilot*, 56-60.

Nunnally, J.C. (1978). *Psychometric theory* (2nd ed.). New York: McGraw-Hill.

Panina, D.Y.(2002). Effects of group cohesiveness and procedural fairness context on the performance and stress of electronically monitored individuals. *Dissertation Abstracts International: Section B. Sciences and Engineering*, 63(6B), 3069. (Doctoral Dissertation, Rutgers University, 2002).

Pfleiderer, E.M., & Chidester, T.R. (2011). *Establishing the reliability and validity of the Perceptions of Flight Operations Quality Assurance (PFOQA) questionnaire* (Report No. DOT/FAA/AM-11/6). Washington, DC: FAA Office of Aerospace Medicine.

Schroeder, D., Bailey, L., Pounds, J., & Manning, C. (2006). *A human factors review of the operational error literature.* (Report No. DOT/FAA/AM-06/21). Washington, DC: FAA Office of Aerospace Medicine.

Tabachnick, B.G., & Fidell, L.S. (2006). *Using multivariate statistics* (5th ed.). New York: HarperCollins.

Warwick, G. (2009, November 30). Evidence of progress: Using flight-recorder data from accidents and incidents could help civil pilots "train as they fly." *Aviation Week & Space Technology*, p. 57.

Westin, A.F. (1992). Two key factors that belong in the macroergonomic analysis of electronic monitoring: employee perceptions of fairness and the climate of organizational trust or distrust. *Applied Ergonomics, 23*(1), 35-42.

Zumbo, B.D., & Zimmerman, D.W. (1993). Is the selection of statistical methods governed by level of measurement? *Canadian Psychology, 34*, 390-400.

Appendix A

Perceptions of Flight Operations Quality Assurance (PFOQA) Online Survey

Please respond to each item by indicating your level of agreement with the statement.

#	Statement	Strongly Agree	Agree	Disagree	Strongly Disagree	No Opinion
1.	FOQA is a program designed to enhance safety by identifying potential hazards before they result in an accident.	○	○	○	○	○
2.	"Gatekeepers" are the <u>only</u> persons able to access identifying information that associates a pilot or pilots with exceedences.	○	○	○	○	○
3.	I trust management will not misuse FOQA data against individual pilots.	○	○	○	○	○
4.	Flying skills have improved or will improve with a FOQA program in place.	○	○	○	○	○
5.	I worry that FOQA data will be a source of information for enforcement action against pilots.	○	○	○	○	○
6.	I expect FOQA data to be used to take action to correct safety problems.	○	○	○	○	○
7.	I expect FOQA data to be used to improve pilot training.	○	○	○	○	○
8.	I expect FOQA to be used to optimize maintenance.	○	○	○	○	○
9.	I worry that FOQA data will be used for disciplinary actions.	○	○	○	○	○
10.	I expect FOQA data to be used to change cockpit procedures.	○	○	○	○	○
11.	I expect FOQA data to provide our pilot group with useful feedback on our performance.	○	○	○	○	○
12.	I expect FOQA data to be used to change procedures outside our organization (such as in Air Traffic).	○	○	○	○	○
13.	I expect the FOQA program to positively impact the safety of our operations.	○	○	○	○	○
14.	A FOQA program has negatively impacted, or will negatively impact, the morale of our pilots.	○	○	○	○	○
15.	I worry that FOQA data could be released under the Freedom of Information Act.	○	○	○	○	○
16.	I worry that FOQA data could be released through civil litigation.	○	○	○	○	○

Please answer a few questions about your background and experience.

17. What aircraft fleet(s) are you currently flying?
(Please check all that apply.)

18. Where are you based?

19. Please describe your experience with FOQA programs.
(Please check all that apply.)
- ☐ Read industry articles
- ☐ Attended briefings/training regarding FOQA programs
- ☐ Served as a flight crew member on an aircraft actively participating in a FOQA program
- ☐ Participated on an event review committee and/or in an official capacity of program administration
- ☐ Other (Please specify)

20. Have you served as a pilot on an aircraft fleet equipped with FOQA before joining AJW? ○ Yes ○ No

21. Please indicate the cumulative amount of time you have served as a flight crew member on an aircraft actively participating in a FOQA program.
Years ☐ Months ☐

22. What is the highest level of education you completed?
--Click Here--

23. Please tell us anything else you think we should know about your expectations or concerns about FOQA.
(Your unedited comments will be compiled with others and forwarded to AJW.)

Thank you for your participation!

Appendix B

Perceptions of Flight Operations Quality Assurance Questionnaire:
Principal Component Analysis

Principal Components Analysis (PCA) with Varimax rotation converged in three iterations and produced two components with eigenvalues greater than 1. As shown in the rotated component matrix in Table C1, all variables had a loading greater than .60 with at least one of the components. The extracted components accounted for approximately 68% of the variance in the dataset.

Table C1. *Principal Components Analysis Rotated Component Matrix* (*N* = 83)

Perceptions of Flight Operations Quality Assurance (PFOQA) Questionnaire Item	Component	
	1	2
03 I trust management will not misuse FOQA data against individual pilots.	-.74	
05 I worry that FOQA data will be a source of information for enforcement action against pilots.	.85	
09 I worry that FOQA data will be used for disciplinary actions.	.90	
14 A FOQA program has negatively impacted, or will negatively impact, the morale of our pilots.	.66	
15 I worry that FOQA data could be released under the Freedom of Information Act.	.86	
16 I worry that FOQA data could be released through civil litigation.	.80	
01 FOQA is a program designed to enhance safety by identifying potential hazards before they result in an accident.		.68
04 Flying skills have improved or will improve with a FOQA program in place.		.73
06 I expect FOQA data to be used to take action to correct safety problems.		.72
07 I expect FOQA data to be used to improve pilot training.		.80
11 I expect FOQA data to provide our pilot group with useful feedback on our performance.		.86
13 I expect the FOQA program to positively impact the safety of our operations.		.79

Component loadings < .40 not shown.

The proportion of variance a rotated component accounts for is an estimate of its importance (Tabachnick & Fidell, 2006). Components 1 and 2 were nearly equivalent in this regard. Component 1 (Negative Perceptions) had an eigenvalue of 4.24 and accounted for 35% of the variance. Items associated with Component 1 express concerns about data misuse. Component 2 (Positive Expectations) had an eigenvalue of 3.94 and accounted for 33% of the variance. Items associated with Component 2 involved positive expectations about the benefits of FOQA programs.

Perceptions of Flight Operations Quality Assurance (PFOQA) Questionnaire:
Invitation to Participate

 **Federal Aviation
Administration**

Memorandum

Date:

To: All Aviation System Standards Pilots

From: Thomas C. Accardi, Director of Aviation System Standards, AJW-3
Thomas R. Chidester, Manager, Aerospace Human Factors Research Division,
AAM-500

Subject: Perceptions of Flight Operations Quality Assurance Survey

Aviation System Standards is conducting a survey in partnership with the Aerospace Human Factors Research Division, AAM-500, at the Civil Aerospace Medical Institute (CAMI). This is part of a research study to increase our understanding of how Flight Operations Quality Assurance (FOQA) programs are perceived, both by pilots who have first hand experience with them and those who have not. As such, you are in an ideal position to provide valuable information from your own perspective.

The *Perceptions of Flight Operations Quality Assurance* online survey takes approximately 5 minutes to complete. Participation is completely anonymous, which means that no one (not even the research team) will know the name of any pilot who responds. AAM-500 conducts research in support of the Federal Aviation Administration Aviation Safety and Air Traffic organizations. Its research is compliant with 45 CFR Part 46 "Protection of Human Subjects" and FAA Order 9500.25 "Protection of Human Research Subjects," and is conducted under approval of the FAA Institutional Review Board. These regulations protect the confidentiality of participants. In this study, your feedback is both confidential and anonymous. *You will not be asked for your name, and personal identifiers, such as IP addresses, will not be recorded.* We would like to invite you to complete the survey.

Although there is no direct compensation for participating in this study, understanding your expectations, experiences, and concerns is important for making FOQA programs as effective as possible. Your participation constitutes a valuable contribution to the FAA, the aviation community, and the flying public.

If you consent to participate, simply connect to: [URL]

This URL has been given only to Aviation System Standards pilots, and will take you directly to the *Perceptions of Flight Operations Quality Assurance* questionnaire. Please remember that participation is voluntary, so you need only respond to questions you feel comfortable answering and are free to withdraw from participation at any time. This survey has been coordinated with the union.

Appendix D

Perceptions of Flight Operations Quality Assurance (PFOQA) Questionnaire Items:
Frequencies and Percentages

Q1   FOQA is a program designed to enhance safety by identifying potential hazards before they result in an accident.

Response	Frequency	Valid Percent
1	0	0.0
2	4	4.9
3	38	46.3
4	40	48.8
Total	82	100.0

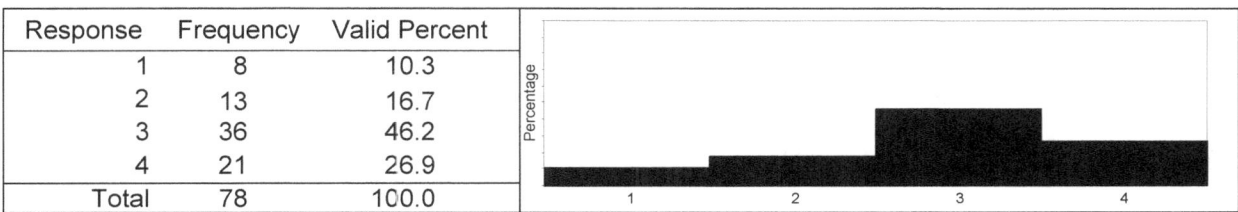

Q2   Gatekeepers are the only persons able to access identifying information that associates a pilot or pilots with exceedances.

Response	Frequency	Valid Percent
1	8	10.3
2	13	16.7
3	36	46.2
4	21	26.9
Total	78	100.0

Q3   I trust management will not misuse FOQA data against individual pilots.

Response	Frequency	Valid Percent
1	12	15.2
2	18	22.8
3	30	38.0
4	19	24.1
Total	79	100.0

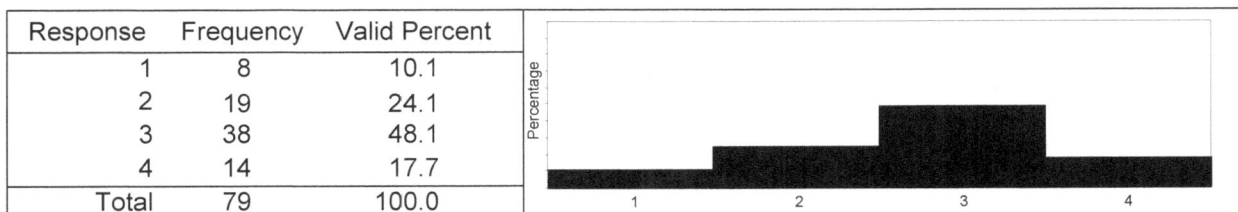

Q4   Flying skills have improved or will improve with a FOQA program in place.

Response	Frequency	Valid Percent
1	8	10.1
2	19	24.1
3	38	48.1
4	14	17.7
Total	79	100.0

1 = Strongly Disagree, 2 = Disagree, 3 = Agree, 4 = Strongly Agree

Q5   I worry that FOQA data will be a source of information for enforcement action against pilots.

Response	Frequency	Valid Percent
1	11	13.8
2	32	40.0
3	27	33.8
4	10	12.5
Total	80	100.0

Q6   I expect FOQA data to be used to take action to correct safety problems.

Response	Frequency	Valid Percent
1	1	1.2
2	4	4.9
3	47	58.0
4	29	35.8
Total	81	100.0

Q7   I expect FOQA data to be used to improve pilot training.

Response	Frequency	Valid Percent
1	1	1.2
2	11	13.4
3	48	58.5
4	22	26.8
Total	82	100.0

Q8   I expect FOQA data to be used to optimize maintenance.

Response	Frequency	Valid Percent
1	6	8.7
2	16	23.2
3	32	46.4
4	15	21.7
Total	69	100.0

Q9   I worry that FOQA data will be used for disciplinary actions.

Response	Frequency	Valid Percent
1	12	15.4
2	28	35.9
3	30	38.5
4	8	10.3
Total	78	100.0

1 = Strongly Disagree, 2 = Disagree, 3 = Agree, 4 = Strongly Agree

Q10   I expect FOQA data to be used to change cockpit procedures.

Response	Frequency	Valid Percent
1	0	0.0
2	5	6.3
3	57	72.2
4	17	21.5
Total	79	100.0

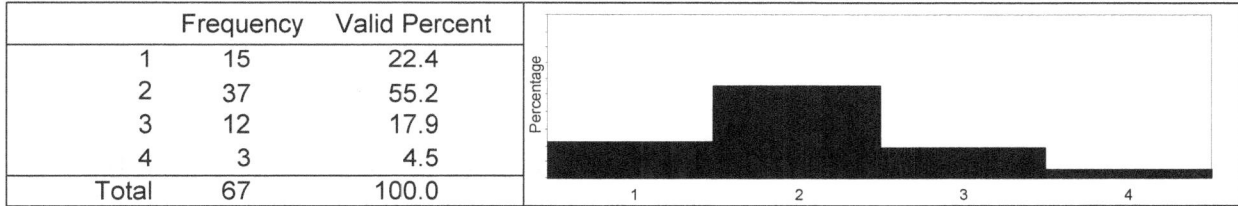

Q11   I expect FOQA data to provide our pilot group with useful feedback on our performance.

Response	Frequency	Valid Percent
1	4	4.9
2	11	13.4
3	45	54.9
4	22	26.8
Total	82	100.0

Q12   I expect FOQA data to be used to change procedures outside our organization (e.g., ATC).

	Frequency	Valid Percent
1	15	22.4
2	37	55.2
3	12	17.9
4	3	4.5
Total	67	100.0

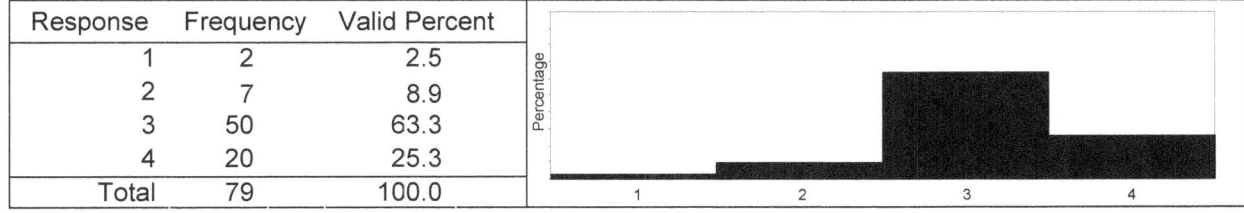

Q13   I expect the FOQA program to positively impact the safety of our operations.

Response	Frequency	Valid Percent
1	2	2.5
2	7	8.9
3	50	63.3
4	20	25.3
Total	79	100.0

1 = Strongly Disagree, 2 = Disagree, 3 = Agree, 4 = Strongly Agree

Q14 A FOQA program has negatively impacted, or will negatively impact, the morale of our pilots.

Response	Frequency	Valid Percent
1	11	14.3
2	43	55.8
3	16	20.8
4	7	9.1
Total	77	100.0

Q15 I worry that FOQA data could be released under the Freedom of Information Act.

Response	Frequency	Valid Percent
1	5	6.9
2	22	30.6
3	35	48.6
4	10	13.9
Total	72	100.0

Q16 I worry that FOQA data could be released through civil litigation.

Response	Frequency	Valid Percent
1	3	4.2
2	16	22.2
3	38	52.8
4	15	20.8
Total	72	100.0

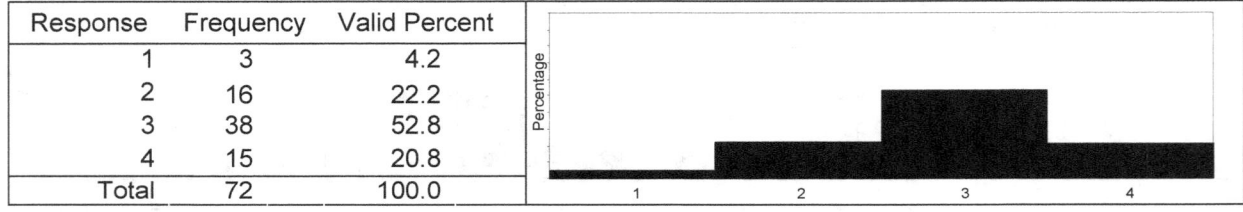

1 = Strongly Disagree, 2 = Disagree, 3 = Agree, 4 = Strongly Agree

www.ingramcontent.com/pod-product-compliance
Lightning Source LLC
Chambersburg PA
CBHW080942290526
45795CB00007BA/2867